Let Go, My Love

Dorothy Gurkin Hellman

Bloch Publishing Company • *New York.*

Table of Contents

Introduction   vii

Acknowledgments   ix

Thanks   xi

In Memoriam   xiii

Part I, Death In Winter   1

Part II, The First Spring and Summer   31

Part III, The Leaves are Falling   59

Part IV, This Year Has Passed   91

Part V, No One Ever Promised Us Tomorrow   121

Index of First Lines   167

Introduction

Three years ago, when my husband died, I struggled to find my own identity, to find myself as a person apart from the one I loved.

My thoughts seemed to race helter-skelter on a collision course. Intrusive. Insistent. Repetitive. A psychological stream of consciousness. I had to write down what I was thinking, what I was feeling. That is how *Let Go, My Love* came to be written.

It is an authentic outpouring of my emotions as I moved from deepest despair to a gradual realization that although I could not forget the past, I need not be trapped by it.

Dorothy Gurkin Hellman

Dorothy Gurkin Hellman

Acknowledgments

To the following:

Lisa Besdin, my editor, for her sensitivity, skill and understanding

Mildred McClosky and Adele Horwitz, for their encouragement and initial assistance

Jerome Davidson, for his overall moral support

—my love and appreciation.

D.G.H.

From Both of Us, Thanks

My family. My children and my greater family. How can I thank you? Jesse, Richard, Gerard. Maria and Joan. Little Stacey Jo, you've helped, too. Bea and Bill. Sylvia and George. Mitz and Herb. Mae and Al. How much you've done. How very much you've done. There are no words.

And our friends. Barbara, dear Barbara. How could we have closed up the office without you? Arnold. Ruth and Raoul. Gisele and Harold. Always there. Mildred and Gerry. Mary and Jo. Elaine and Mel. Bernice and Bob. Shirley, far, but in close touch, each knowing too well how the other feels.

And Jerry. The spiritual and thoughtful words you spoke on that sad, sad day are with me still.

Franklin and Wilma. Cliff and Rhoda. Stan and Bernice. Fred. Bill. Other friends at school.

Our nieces and nephews. Cousins. Aunts. That one dear Uncle. Concerned. Caring.

No matter that you are doctors, lawyers, professors, teachers and such. You've pitched in as plumbers, handymen, cabbies, mechanics and cooks. Nothing has been too much. Nothing was too little.

To each of you I've named, and the many dear friends I haven't, let me say thank you. Thank you all. Very, very much.

From both of us. Thank you. Thanks. Very, very.much.

IN MEMORIAM
TO SIDNEY JESSE HELLMAN

We walked life's path
Together, knowing
Pain and joy
Stumbling somewhat
Finding our way
Creating
Our sons
Loving, dreaming, striving
You were my other self
I did not know at times
Was it you, or I?
It did not matter
We were one
We are one....
Still

Part I

Death in Winter

There's nothing to be said
My love is dead
Can hardly say it
Dead
My love is dead
I am stricken
Stricken
Stricken
As a falling bird
I lift my wings
Try to fly
Want to die
Want to die
I cannot fly
What shall I do
Can't go to you
What shall I do?

I'd have followed you, my love
To go
With you
　　Was what I wanted
But I couldn't leave
　　There were those
　　Who'd grieve
I didn't dare
There were those
　　Who care
I couldn't hurt
　　My loved ones
To go with you
Was what I wanted
But I could not leave
There were those
Who'd grieve
I'd have followed you
You know
But I could not go

Dreary
Weary
But the bells
Have tolled
I must depart
Time to start
My journey
A widow's journey
Feel so cold, so cold
Feel so old, so old
But I must start
My journey
A widow's journey

A plaintive call
To all
Who mourn
Chant
A mourning song
A mourning song
Chant
A mourning song
With me
It had to be
It had to be
Chant
A mourning song
With me
We loved and lost
So great a cost
But it had to be
It had to be
Chant
A mourning song
With me

We are mortal
We are mortal
We are mortal
Oh woman
Your man
Was mortal
Nothing could be done
About that

Who am I
To be the favored one
Why should I
Be spared
Such sorrow

Since Time began
Till Time does end
Tomorrow or tomorrow
Or tomorrow
There's been
And will be
Sorrow

Today
Or tomorrow
Sorrow
Why should I
Be spared
Sorrow

Sometimes
I wish I had been born a flower
A flower lives a life of beauty
Gives joy to others
Fades quickly
Feels no pain
Soon dies

A flower
Wish I had been born a flower
I would live a life of beauty
Give joy to others
Fade quickly
Feel no pain
Soon die

That old, old clock
He liked it so
How does it know
Not to go
That Life stopped

It seems to know
Not to go
The other clocks go on
Just as they did before
Don't seem to know
There's been a change

Strange
But that old, old clock
He liked it so
It seems to know
Not to go
Just seems to know
Not to go

Turned in the M.D. plates
Changed the registration on the car
Long lines today
  Bureaucracy
  Brusque
  Cold
  Impersonal
  Routine
  Just another number
  Routine
There was no other course
Struck full force
Biting
Fighting
Memories
Difficult day
A very difficult day
Turned in those M.D. plates
  Finality
  Full force
  FINALITY

I must get back to school
There are my classes to be met
Cannot really let
Too much time go by
Must try
Just hope that I can cope
With my despair
When I am there
And not forget
My students
To be met
Back at school

There are records to keep. Records to keep. File cabinets. Folders. Clearly marked. What's coming in. What's going out. What's due. What's new. Records to keep. I've got to know. Which way to go.

Records to keep. Records to keep.

People who live alone have long since learned that. It's nothing new. Must learn too. Records to keep.

And the house. How does one manage? Leaky faucets. A flood in the basement. That crack in the wall. Storm windows. Gushing toilet. Good grief, all thumbs. All thumbs. Why didn't I ever learn about those things.

Why didn't I share those tasks?

Not too late to learn. The house is there. I'm there. I must learn. So much to learn. So much to learn.

Weird feeling. Coming home alone at night. Not afraid. Somehow, not at all afraid. Not really. But coming home alone after all the years of coming home together, seems so strange. Weird feeling. To open the door. Come in alone. To a quiet house.

Quiet house. Quiet, quiet house. Must turn that radio on. Get it on the minute I walk into the house alone. News. Lectures. Discussions. Anything. Doesn't matter. Just get that radio on.

Or T.V. Some good programs. Ought to check them out. Keep forgetting. Must remember to check them out. Must not let the house be too quiet. Too alone. Not now.

Radio. T.V. Listen to someone's voice. Break up the quiet. Won't feel so much alone. In the quiet house.

Should I move? No, not yet. Now now, if at all. The quiet is devastating. The once lively house so still, empty. But there are memories. Why run away?

I wander from room to room. Look around. The treasured objects accumulated through the years. Mementos. Here and there. Favorite etchings. Books. I touch his pipe. His chair.

The house still echoes with the music that he loved. I hold his violin. The bow needs restringing. I put it away. Don't know for whom. But I put the violin away.

I go through old pictures. Tears running down my cheeks. Hard to see. So many, many pictures, whatever should be done with all those pictures? Albums. Put them in albums. Duplicates? Throw them away. The pictures stare at me. I stare at the pictures.

I listen to some favorite records. Tears. Again, tears. Why not? Cry. Yes, cry.

Will there ever again be laughter? Real spontaneous laughter? Natural laughter? Is it possible?

In the meantime, I wander from room to room. Days pass. Nights. Weeks. Can't remember how many.

I wander from room to room.

15.

If only there were someone at home to talk to,
to fuss over a little. Someone with whom to share
the thoughts of each day. "Guess what happened
today," or "How did it go, today?"

When the boys left, one by one, it was lonely.
We missed them. But we had each other. And we
looked forward to the times they would come home.
Much as we adored having them back, we were
almost a little glad, while sad, to see them go.
We rather liked the peace and quiet. Being
alone together, after all those years.

With one stroke, all that's gone. Now day
changes into night, and night into day. There's
no one to say "Guess what happened today", no
one to ask "How'd things go, today?".

No one to ask.

Hard to fall asleep. I wake up often. Wake up early. Don't care. Should I care?

Napoleon, they say, slept four or five hours. Heard it was so for Eleanor Roosevelt. Golda Meir, too.

Who said we need so much sleep, anyway?

Mind over matter. Does it matter?

But the days are so long, the nights longer. Days. Nights. Long. Long. Long.

Longing.

Aimless days. Vacuous nights.

Long, listless days.

Quiet, lonely nights.

Long, long, long.

Longing.

Have to go through so many things. Personal effects.
What to keep. What to discard.

The army clothes. The army helmet. Shirt, jacket,
insignia. Can't discard these, of course.

Sorting. Going through everything. Tears me apart.
His clothes are gone now, most anyway. But so many
personal things. Where to start. What to do?

The old diplomas. The hard-earned coveted
achievements.

"Fellow of the American College of Surgeons".

"Diplomate of the American Board of Surgery."

"Fellow of the Academy of Medicine"

So many. So hard to come by. So hard to know what
to do.

Save the most important.

But can't help wondering. Some day, where will
they all be?

Is there a graveyard for old honors and diplomas?

Am tired. Exhausted. Don't feel like going anywhere.
Don't feel like doing anything.

Must not feel this way. Can't afford to feel this way.
A rut. Must not get into a rut. Keep moving. Must keep
moving. Try to be with others more. Accept more
invitations. Invite people here.

Might feel more alive. Let others know I'm still
alive. Might even convince myself after awhile. That
I'm still alive.

Hear the wind
Howling so
See the snow
See the snow
   "Too cold to snow"
   He used to say
Wonder what he'd say
Today

I must learn to build a little wall
A little wall
A little wall
When they call
Or when we meet
Accidentally
On the street
"How are you managing?" they say
Or
"How are you getting on today?"
Just learn to say
"O.K. O.K.
I'm feeling fine today"
Must learn to build a little wall
When they call
Or when we meet
Accidentally
On the street

NO MATTER HOW HARD I TRY
THERE'S NO USE PRETENDING
IT HURTS!
IT HURTS!
GOD, HOW IT HURTS!

I see, and don't see. I hear, and don't hear. It's like sitting in a darkened theater, watching, listening, yet at times feeling far away, so far away. I'm with it, yet out of it, part of it, yet apart from it, can't quite escape the kaleidoscopic thoughts that catapult themselves this way and that wherever I turn, pervasive, intruding.

Concentrate, can't concentrate, always back to the same thought.

No one but you.

No one but you.

No one but you.

So I see, but don't see. I hear, but don't hear. Away, far, far away. With it, yet out of it. Can't escape.

You.

Seems
I can't help
Brooding
It creeps up on me
Silently
Like a cat
   SCAT!
Please
  Go away
Please
  Go away
I have to stop
This brooding

Despair
Despair
Rudderless
    Like a sailboat
    Drifting
What course should I take?
How can I get there?
    Come now
    ENOUGH!
Too rough
    ENOUGH!

Drowning
Sometimes I think
I'm drowning
Undertow
Of sorrow
Pulling me
Down
Think I'll drown
Of sorrow
Drown
Of sorrow

Death
You dealt such cards
My soul is now in shards
   Fragments. Shattered. Shards.
My soul that once was whole
Is now in shards
I am undone
Sun
You up there in brassy splendor
Tell me, do you ever tender
To a soul in shards?
Send your strongest forces down
Into my being
Freeing me from fragmentation
Freeing me from stagnation
Fire my soul anew
A patched up soul
With some semblance
That is whole
Is better than a soul
In shards

Oh, my love
My dearest love
Where do I turn
I yearn
So much for you
My love
There is no way
To say
The loss I feel
Where do I turn
I yearn
So much for you
What. shall I do
What shall I do
I yearn
So much for you

I PROMISE
I PROMISE
I'LL TRY NOT TO CRY
MY DARLING, MY DARLING
I'LL TRY NOT TO CRY

Part II

The First Spring and Summer

STRANGE to think of going to dinner alone
STRANGE to think of going to the theater alone
STRANGE to think of going to the museum alone
STRANGE to think of going to the opera alone, the
   ballet
STRANGE to think of traveling alone
STRANGE to think of doing alone
   What we always did together
   Will it ever seem less strange?

How much I wish my love could have lived. For his sake, if not for mine. If only he could have lived.

What are others thinking? Do I really care what others are thinking? I do care. Don't want to show the way I feel. Don't want to reveal how crushed I am, how sad and lonely. Must not show how I feel. Must not reveal how I feel.

Cover the sadness. Don a mask. Choose one with a smile. There. That one over there. That will do for awhile. That one with the little smile.

Wear that mask.

Put on that mask.

Your son, Mom. My husband. So intertwined these many years. So caring. Now when we're together, we pretend. Hard to pretend.

We talk of this. Of that. Chit-chat. Superficial chit-chat. Mustn't strike too sensitive a chord. So we chatter. Meaningless chatter. Inconsequential chatter.

We both pretend. As though it hadn't happened. As though it were as before. Your son. My husband.

Inside we are silently weeping. We both know it. Silently weeping.

But we pretend.

35.

Absent-minded. So absent-minded. Never before, this absent-minded. Can't recall what I did or put down just a few moments ago. Losing my memory? Temporary state of confusion? Disorientation? Past events and present merge. Memories and current happenings fuse together. Hard to know which is which. They march in phalanx. Wheel around. Feint off. Come together sharply. Recede. Slowly. Merge again.

Stop it. Stop this nonsense. Time to get my bearings. Old army of memories. Confused. Must march ahead.

Such confusion. Confusion, will you tire of yourself? And go away?

Sometimes I feel
So droopy
Like a pair
Of droopy drawers
Look so silly
Feel so sad
How can one
Feel silly
And sad
At the same time?
   Droopy drawers
   Droopy drawers
Look so silly
Feel so sad
So sad

Not well. Don't feel so well. Swollen glands. Fever. Aches and pains. Don't much care how I feel, but it's so unpleasant to be ill, alone at home, without him. He took such care. He always took such good care. Made me better. Always made me feel so much better. He had that touch. And cared so much. Made me better.

No fun, this, being ill. Drags me down. Down. Don't like being sick.

Get well. Might as well. Get well.

Just knowing there won't be the key in the lock, the cheery "Hi" I used to wait for, makes all the difference when I'm home. Alone. All the difference. Big, big difference.

I try to read, but my attention span is erratic. I read the same sentence again. And again. A paragraph takes hours. Or so it seems. My mind wanders. Wanders.

It takes working at. Living alone. After so many years. Can't just suddenly adjust. Or expect instantaneous miracles. Patience. Patience. PATIENCE.

Must learn not to expect that key in the lock. Learn to live alone. No key in the lock.

When you were little ones
My sons
We loved you so
Did you know
We loved you so?

Loved you then
Love you still
Loved you then
Always will

Now when you come home, we're all so glad to be
together. But there is a little strangeness. We care so
much about each other. But there is a little strangeness.
I can tell. You can tell, too. We're not quite relaxed.
What should we say? What should we do?
    Guess it takes time. Time to get used to our new
roles. Home. Without Dad. It must be very strange
for you to come home. See Mom. Without Dad.

His presence is everywhere....this room, or that. In everything I touch. So real, it seems that any moment he will speak. I almost believe that this must be some mad nightmare, that soon I'll hear that loved, loving voice reassuring, comforting.

"Whatever have you been dreaming? There now, it's over. Over."

But no. It is not so. The forlorn hope fades. His presence had seemed so real.

Was it Reality?

Or fantasy?

I cannot tell.

Spring
Seems barren
This year
   Spring,
     Have you sprung?
So lifeless
So desolate

Is the desolateness my own blurred perspective?
Am I refusing to accept this change in my life? Somehow,
I'm going to have to face it. Face it squarely. Stop
dodging. Face it squarely.

What has happened to my character? Where's my
courage? Where's my discipline? How shall I think? How
shall I collect my thoughts?

I remember *Pollyanna*, the Glad Girl. She always found
something to be glad about. "It could have been worse,"
she used to say.

And what about Scarlett? Scarlett O'Hara. When there
were unpleasant situations she always said, "I'll think
about it tomorrow."

What can I be glad about? That he didn't suffer? I'll
think about it tomorrow. NO.

Face it. I must face it.
Broken refrain.
Face it.

Wool gathering
Must stop
Wool gathering
  Mind wandering
  Time squandering
Must stop
Wool gathering
  Gather myself together
Where's my pride?
Mustn't hide
  Hold my head a little higher
  Walk a little taller
Now's the time
If ever
  Stop wool-gathering
Where's my pride?
Mustn't hide
  Hold my head a little higher
  Walk a little straighter
  Walk a little taller
Now's the time
If ever

He had that zest for life
He knew just what to do
No dull moments
Not for him
He would not have it so
   When to work
   When to play
   What to save
   For another day
He knew just what to do
He had that zest for life
   Now I
   Who was his wife
   Must find that zest for life
   Must find that zest for life

Think I'll take up bridge again. Used to play. Way back. But then there wasn't time. So much to do. So much else to do. No time for bridge.

Now there's time. Plenty of time. Too much time. Bridge. Build a bridge. Bridge may help me cross from old to new. Play bridge.

I must slowly feel my way. Try some new things.

One's family may be the world's best. One's friends, the same. Surely, mine are! Still no one, family nor friends, can overcome this trauma for me. There are things one has to do alone. Work things through alone. Find one's way, alone.

The way. The WAY. TAO. Old Chinese philosophy. The Way.

The Way. Nobody can do it for me. Nobody. Must find my own way. Try new things. Make mistakes. But must slowly find my own way.

Haven't played tennis for years. Many years. Why not start again? I won't try to fly over the court like an eighteen year old. Might fall or collapse. And look sort of silly. Feel even sillier.

Might get tendonitis. Oh well, could get it without playing. Stop putting up roadblocks. Might as well play. It would be fun to play. Play.

Find some kind soul who'll take me on. What about lessons? Anything wrong with that? Do it right. Take some lessons. Life for me certainly seems full of lessons. Should take some lessons.

I knew it
I blew it!
On the tennis court today
What a way to play!
I knew it
I blew it!
On the tennis court today
Oh well
Tomorrow's another day
To learn
To play

First time in New York alone, without you. Wanted to go back to some of our favorite spots. Wanted to see what New York was like, without you. So I went alone.

Walked. Walked. Walked. Block after block. Walked. Didn't stop. Walked. Walked some more. Couldn't decide what to do. Without you.

Tired. Back home. Wondering. Why did I just walk and walk?

Perhaps that's just how it had to be. The first time alone in New York.

Without you.

Alone.

The weekends. So difficult. Weekends. Our weekends had been so special. More time for us to be together. Lincoln Center. Concerts. Opera. Ballet. Theater. There were galleries. Museums. So much to choose from. So much to do.

And there were weekends on the water. We loved to just be together. On the water.

Some weekends we'd take a drive. Here. Or there. Didn't matter where. As long as we had each other.

Now the weekends come and go. In monotonous succession. No matter what is planned. With whom. No matter what I do.

On weekends I'm going to pretend it's Tuesday. From now on. Pretend it's Tuesday. An ordinary Tuesday.

Drifting
Again
Drifting
Like a straw
Buffeted
This way
Or that
Not sure
Whether to go
Upstream
Or down
Drifting
Like a straw
With the current
With the wind

Be still, my soul
Don't restless be
You have to learn
To live with me...

Everyone says Time is the answer. Give it time. Wait and see. Time. Must be true. True for others. So many others. Must be true.

Still too soon for me to know. Does the pain ever go away? Perhaps it becomes less searing. Dull pain one learns to live with, like a nagging toothache acting up now and then.

Perhaps the pain is ever the same. Only I will change. Make some sort of adjustment. Slow. Subtle. Develop a shield. A little shield which insulates the pain. Develop some sort of pain tolerance. Some equilibrium to balance it out.

Thoughts still so poignant. Pain still so deep. Memories still so persistently there. But they tell me Time is the answer.

Time *has* to be the answer.

I'm home
School's out
The summer's ahead

Know what?
I dread
The summer ahead

There's so much rain
There's so much pain
There's too much sun
What's to be done?

Where should I go?
I do not know

Once eagerly awaited summer months. Now, what to
do. Go somewhere. Escape. Nonsense. Why? Anyway,
where? Some strange place? No. Don't want to go. Can't
decide. Go over possibilities. Think things through. See
what's best to do.

Think it's best to stay. At first, anyway. Just stay. Stay
home. Learn how it is to garden alone. Learn to sit
outside alone. Learn to listen to the sounds of the
summer night alone. Learn to get used to his presence-
absence alone.

Must start the summer alone.

Weeds
More weeds
In my garden
  "Mistress Mary, quite contrary
  How does your garden grow?"
I know
That mine
Grows weeds
Widow's weeds
For all the seeds
I planted
I just see
Weeds
Widow's weeds
That's what I see
In my garden

Oh well, laugh. Laugh if you will. A grown person to
be locked out. Locked out of her house. How careless.
How careless can one be. Left water in the kettle. Kettle
on the stove. Boiling. Boiling away.
And I was locked out.
Locked out.
How could I
Get locked out?
That's how things are these days.
Locked out.
Good thing I left a key with my neighbor.
Better to be locked in.
Than locked out.

Everyone has been so kind
But now I see
It's up to me
To find the key
I've been locked out
Know what it's about
To be locked out
Scared
Bared
To the soul
No key
But now I see
No one but me
Has the key
To go inside
My soul
And make it whole
No one but me
Has the key

At times, this past winter and spring, my mind would suddenly go blank. Completely blank. Right in the classroom. In the midst of a discussion.

Would find myself wondering. Why am I here? What questions had I asked? What were the answers?

But those moments passed. Don't know if any of my students knew. But those moments passed.

Now the summer is ending. Soon it will be time to go back. Start a new school year. Guess I'm sort of looking forward to going back.

To my friends.

To my classroom.

To the challenges. Of teaching.

Each night
When I am in bed
Lights out
Ready to fall asleep
Whenever it strikes Sleep's fancy
I put out my hand
As we always did
To say one last good night
I put out my hand
As we always did
To say good night
To say good night

IF I COULD JUST PHONE YOU
SAY HELLO
ASK HOW YOU ARE
IF I COULD JUST PHONE YOU

Part III

The Leaves are Falling

Leaves
Orange, red, yellow, green
Every color to be seen
Tumbling down
Making a bed
Of leaves
Shaking one
Who grieves
I pick up leaves
I pick up leaves
First one, then another
Smother
A cry
Why couldn't you be
Here to see
Along with me
The autumn leaves
Be here with me
To see
The autumn leaves

Widow
Never thought I'd be a widow
Thought that
Somehow
Someday
Some way
We could face
Death
Together
At some uncertain time and place
The two of us would face
Death
Together
No journey alone
Destination unknown
But go together
As we did in life
Go
Together

My heart
Beats monotonously
  Beat!
  Beat!
  Beat!
Is that all
It is good for
Shouldn't it
Open up a little now?
Just a little?
Is it just there
To keep that
  Beat!
  Beat!
  Beat!

It's almost dinner time. Don't feel like cooking.
Not much appetite. Don't feel like eating out.

Are the department stores open tonight? It's
Thursday, I think. Yes, it's Thursday. Good. They're
open. That's what I'll do. Go to the department
stores. What do I need? Can't remember. What
should I buy? That doesn't matter, either. Something
or nothing. Doesn't matter. Why go? Don't know.

Just to go.

Makes me feel better to be part of that hectic
bustling. Everyone in the store seems so lively. To
have a purpose. They laugh. Talk. Some even yell
at their kids:

"Didn't I tell you not to move from this spot, didn't
I tell you?"

Don't much care what they're saying. Or buying. Or
trying on. It's just better to walk around. Hear the noisy
chatter. Stop at a counter. Or a rack of clothes.

So go shopping. Even if there's nothing I want to
buy. Not hungry tonight? Dreary dinner time? The
stores are open tonight.

That's where I'll go.

I am afraid
Of being a fifth wheel
With our friends
Still married, still together
Afraid to go with them
Afraid of being a fifth wheel

"Nonsense"
They say
"Nonsense
We know too well
We've lost him
Must we lose you, too?"

Afraid of being a fifth wheel
But my friends
My dear, dear friends
They know
Just how I feel
Fifth wheel
They know
Just how
I feel

Those neighbors in the stucco house
Across the way
They're peeking

Peeking
Not to pry
Not to see me cry

Seeking
To see if I'm O.K.
If there's anything I need
Today
To see at night
If I'm all right

Seeking
That's why they are peeking
Those neighbors in the stucco house
Across the way

I'm going off to the library, that's what. Hundreds and hundreds of books, on any subject, fiction or non-fiction. I ought to look up how to fix this, make that.

Perhaps I'll take out a record, or maybe even listen to some new recording there. Should I go downstairs to the Art Exhibit? I think there's a lecture, too.

No, I'll just go through some magazines. But there are so many. I don't know which one to look at.

What book shall I take out? What subject?

Can't make up my mind. All throughout this year. Every time I go to the library, I can't make up my mind.

But I've made up my mind to go to the library. Don't care if I don't take out a record, don't care if I don't read through the magazines. I'll go to the library anyway. Good place to go.

Thanksgiving
Always loved Thanksgiving
Without him now
What shall we do
To get through
This Thanksgiving?

   Let's have the clan
   Do what we can
   To find some cheer
   Without him here
   He'd want it so
   I know
   I know
Always loved Thanksgiving
But he's not here
Must find some cheer
Have the clan
Do what we can
He'd want it so
I know

Unexpectedly, just like that, tears come.
When I think I have everything under control. Then.....
A song. A word. A look. And suddenly those tears just
come.
A roomful of people.
I walk out. So no one can see.
Tears. Uncontrollable tears.
Feel so sagging. Like a broken-down spinach
soufflé. The kind that looks fine from the outside.
But turns out to be thin. All froth. Little substance.
Lots of puff. No real stuff.
Tears.
Uncontrollable tears.

I'm such a dodo bird
I make so many mistakes
I drop
Drop
Drop
Clumsy
Forget
I'm a blank
Feel foolish
Scatterbrained
Things I know so well
Can't remember
  Don't be a dodo bird
  DODO BIRD
  DODO BIRD
  DODO BIRD
  Don't be a dodo bird
Will I ever
Be a whole person
Again?

There's still a long way to go. I thought that I was fine. Getting my second wind. Getting pretty far ahead. Winning the game.

It is not so easy.

Back in Newark, many years ago, we played a game. A game to see who could get to the other side of the street. The leader would call out:

"Take three giant steps forward."

Everybody did.

Then the leader would call "Stop!"

Those still moving would be slapped with a penalty.

"Take two giant steps backwards."

So we all played the game, hoping to be the first to get to the other side. To become the new leader.

I used to play that game quite well.

It seems as though I'm playing that game now. Guess it will take a little while before I can get to the other side. Play it well enough.

To win.

Take a walk. I must take a walk. Walk. Walk. Walk.
Take a walk.
When I walk along, I can remember.
When I walk along, I can forget.
Walk. Walk. Walk.
I can plan while I walk.
I can think while I walk.
I can dream while I walk.
In winter it is cold, piercing. The wind whips me
this way and that. I cannot go too far.
In spring, the trees and flowers are friendly. I am
encouraged to go on.
In summer, the birds are calling, calling, calling.
In fall, the russet leaves are falling, falling, falling.
Walk. Walk. Take a walk.
A walk to remember.
A walk to forget.
A walk to walk to walk to walk. Walk.

Pleasant
To be asked
Somewhere
But when I'm there
It is not where
I want to be
Restless urge
Comes over me
To run
   "Good night. Thanks so much.
   Good night. Lovely time.
   Now I must run."
Can't stay too long
In any one place
Must run
   Run where?
Don't care
   But still I know
That I must run

Always a circle. So many advances. So many retreats. The world spins on its axis. Centuries pass.

Progress
Setbacks
Spinning in a circle
  Discoveries
  Destruction
Spinning in a circle
  Energy
  Pollution
Spinning in a circle
  Land on the moon
  Come back to earth
Spinning in a circle
  The earth is a circle
  Spinning in a circle

Am I in the middle?
Caught in the middle?
Caught in the middle of the circle?
No way to get out?

Afraid people will criticize me if I seem happy?
Widows mourn, they say. Widows scorn laughter. No
time for gladness. Must show sadness.
   Must I feel guilty if I smile? Or laugh? Or sound
O.K.? Am I afraid of what they'll say?
   "Look. She's forgotten. So soon. Look at her.
Smiling, laughing. She's forgotten so soon."
   Do I really seem happy? To them? Don't really
know. Is it a pose? Who knows? There is a pose. Of
course there is a pose. A pose to cover sadness. Each
laugh. Each smile. Each thing I do. It's a pose. To
cover sadness.
   Sometimes the pose falls right on its nose. The sadness
just comes through. Each thing I do. The sadness
just comes through.

Cover that layer of sadness
With some veneer
Of gladness
Smile
That Mona Lisa smile
While
Underneath
A wreath
Of grief
Veneer
So thin
Shows through
Must do
More coatings

Off
Take off my mask
I'm home
Back home
Alone
Take off my mask
There's no one here
To see
But me

Looks as though
It's going to pour
For
The skies are leaden
Drab and grey
Think it's going to pour today
   Pour
   Pour
   Pour today
   Drab and grey
   So drab and grey
   Think it's going to pour today
It will not bother me, you see
For I am dull and drab today
Leaden, dull and drab today
So let it pour
Pour
Pour
Let it pour
Today

Pain so deep
Pain so sharp
Hard to breathe
Pressing so
Will it ever go?
Sharp, so deep
How can I keep
My head up?

Time
Everyone says Time
Will heal

But I feel
So pained
So strained
Time
What can you do
To pull me through
This pain?
Others have gotten by
Can I?

Complaining?
No sense
In complaining
What good
Does it do
There's no sense
In complaining
What does it do?
Stop
Complaining

What did I do today?
Let's see. Let's see.
What did I do today

   I ran up the stairs
   And down the stairs
   Ran up the stairs
   And down the stairs
    Up
    Down
    Up
    Down
I ran up the stairs
And down the stairs
That's what I did
Today

There's something I must tell you
Something I must say
No matter you have gone away
There's something
I must say
My heart keeps beating
Beating
Keeps beating out a rhyme
I love you
Love you
Love you
Love you for all time

So many times each day
So many times at night
I say some little word
Or think some special thought
For you alone, my dearest
I go about my tasks
Talk, or laugh, as it might be
But always
You are with me
Whatever it might be
Always you are with me
Whatever it might be

Outside the gate
While I wait
I look around
At the people bound
On this flight
Who otherwise might never meet
Would pass each other on the street
But here they smile
And chat awhile
"No delay," they say
Soon we will board
And wing our way
Right toward the clouds
I sit very still
I have not found the will
To smile or talk awhile
Spirits low and so
I'll just look around
At all these people bound
With me
In flight

I dare you
I double dare you
Whimpering self-pity
Lurking within me
Show yourself
I would confront you
Your stalking
Shadow
Threatens me
I will not have it so
I am resolved
Come out
Face me
I dare you
And then I...I...
Well, come out
I dare you
Double dare you

Staring out at the Pacific Ocean. Seems more placid to me than the Atlantic. Or is it that I feel more placid at this moment?

Here, in Santa Cruz, we're having a lovely picnic on the beach. White wine and chicken. Talking. Watching the stones being washed up on the beach. Myriads of stones.

Do stones know when they are washed up?

I'm going to bring some of the stones home with me as a reminder. Even washed up stones can be picked up.

Be of some use again.

The ocean. I love the ocean. I like to see the waves leaping back and forth.

Playing leapfrog.

Playing leapfrog.

Dynamic water. What is it saying?

Hypnotic. Moving. Surging.

Now still. Tranquilizing.

Mild water. Calm water.

Wild water. Angry water.

Inscrutable water.

Deep. Deep. Deep.

Deep water.

The ocean.

Imponderable.

I love the ocean.

It's therapy.

For me.

Ebb and flow
Ebb and flow
Like the tides
My moods
Come and go
Up, down
High, low
Like the tides
Ebb and flow

What choices do I have?
  Cower?
  Crawl?
  Cry?
None, really
None of these
No, he would not have it so
  I must take hold
  Unfold
  This new chapter
  In my life
  Adapt my ways
  To this new phase
No other choice
None
Really

KEEP THOSE SPIRITS UP
 HOW THEY FLAG
 HOW THEY SAG
OH, KEEP THOSE SPIRITS UP!

Part IV

This Year Has Passed

This year has passed at last. I did not think it would, and except that it brought me Stacey, I'd have removed it from my life. But this year has passed. At last. This sad, sad year has passed.

Now I have Stacey. First little grandchild. Enchanting. Captivating. Already love you so, Stacey Jo.

He would have been wild about you. And you about him. But it couldn't be. You were not meant to know each other.

Mustn't think about that. Not fair to brood about that. No regrets for what couldn't be. Must just be grateful you are here. Such a dear. Little Stacey Jo. So pleased to know you. So lucky to have you. Stacey Jo. I'm lucky to have you, Stacey Jo.

Look. It's sleeting
It's snowing
Hail is beating
Wind is blowing
Little snatches
Icy patches
So no tennis today
Can't play tennis today
Why take a chance
Can see at a glance
It's sleeting, it's snowing
Hail's beating, wind's blowing
No tennis today
Come now, what's a little snow?
Of course I can go
Miss tennis?
Snow's no menace
What's a little snow?
Of course I can go
Play tennis today

Sometimes I do some cross stitching on the sampler
I started over a year ago. It's nowhere near being
finished. Sometimes I do some gros point. On that
tennis racquet cover I was given. Sometimes I just
sit at the machine, sewing. Mending. Fixing. Nothing
much. But I sit at the machine. And sew. Stitch. Stitch.
Again. Stitch. Sew.

Someday I'm going to finish the sampler. The racquet
cover, too. And I'll still sew. What, I don't know.

But for now, I just like to stitch. Now and then.
Stitch. Now and then. Sew.

My mind can wander as I stitch, stitch, stitch.
Wander as I sew.

Those old brass train lamps
On the wall
I recall
When we found them
In Charleston

Old French train lamps
Must have seen so much

I touch them now
As I recall
The time, the place
My thoughts race
Back
To that sunny day
We found them
In Charleston

Thinking back about my education. Had some great courses. So many, many courses. Never enough.

Didn't take enough.

Wonder if the catalogue listed a course on widowhood? Preparation for widowhood. W402 PREPARATION FOR WIDOWHOOD. Graduate students only. Prerequisite: LOVE, COMMITMENT, MARRIAGE.

Was there ever such a course? Should I have looked? Would I have taken it?

Probably not.

Now I must take my own course.

Widowhood.

I learned to cook for you. From the very first, you'd
say "This is great." So I learned to cook for you.
One night, I remember, you got up from the dinner
table, went for your camera. You liked the way the
swordfish looked on the plate. The sprinkling of
red paprika, lemony-vermouth sauce. You liked the
bright green of the broccoli, the yellow corn on the
cob. Red tomatoes, peeking out from a tossed salad.
   You said it was a picture. So you took a picture.
   That's why I learned to cook for you.

At times
I'd be waiting for you
Ready to go
Off to visit friends
Perhaps
Or see a show

And then you'd call
    "Too, ill
    That patient is too ill
    Sorry,
    But we just can't go
    You know"

At times
It made me mad
But now
I'm very glad
That you did call
We really couldn't go
That patient was too ill
You know
We really couldn't go

There were moments of anger
Not all sweetness and light
Once in a great while
There'd be a fight
No fight really, perhaps a harsh word
And then we'd laugh
It was so absurd
    There were things to do
    And places to go
    With much to say
    Along the way
So those moments of anger
Didn't last very long
Neither cared really
Who was right or wrong
    Because both of us knew
    How much we cared
    Each of us knew
    How much we shared

You looked into my eyes
  And knew
How I was feeling
What I was thinking
No fooling you
No fooling you

You looked into my eyes and knew
No words
No need
Indeed

You looked into my eyes
And knew
You knew
No fooling you

Part of what I am
You made me
Part of what I see
Will always be
Through your eyes
How much you showed me
How much you showed me
I listen
I look
I see
What you have shown me

Close
So close
Perhaps
We were too close
But if there were
A second chance
To live with you
Once more
I know I'd choose
To live with you
As before
As we did
As we were
Close
So close
Close

How long the evenings are
How far removed
From just one year ago
How far removed
In time and space
I did not know
One year ago
That I would face
Such long, long nights
Without you
A year's gone by
What has changed?
The nights are still so long
So very, very long
Without you

I'm still in love
With you
No matter you are dead
When all is said
I'm still in love with you
No matter what I do
No one....But you....
I don't regret
I can't forget
I'm still in love
With you
No matter you are dead
When all is said
I'm still in love
With you
So much in love
With you

Remarry
Remarry
They say
But why should I
Remarry?
More people
Are living alone
Than ever before
Why should I
Remarry?

I go through the motions
I say the expected words
I nod
I smile
But all the while
I am more
An inside person
More than before
Outside
I am another person
Will there ever
Really be
An outside me
Like inside?
One and the same
An outside-inside
Person

I am lonely
Family, friends
And still
I am lonely
Will I ever free myself
Of being married to the past?
Beloved, you still hold me
Despite your death
You hold me
In life
I can't forget
I was your wife
Can't forget
Not yet, not yet
Can't forget

It is creeping up again
The pain
Like a fog
Suddenly it's there
I cannot see
What is to be
That pain
Creeping up
Again
Can't see ahead
Dread
The haze
The maze
Of pain
Creeping up
Again

This void within me
So colossal
It engulfs
My very being
What is left?
It would seem
That what is left
Is a very little person
Indeed
A very little person
Indeed

The sky is very blue today. Azure blue. That sky is in
a world all its own.
　The sky is blue today. Very blue. Vast. So vast. Why
do I feel so small? A little panicky. Feel so small. A
little panicky. Not at all sure why.
　The sky is very blue today. I, too, am very blue
today. Feel so small. Blue. And small.

Let me through
Please
What I am carrying
Is very heavy
It is my heart
Locked in my past
Caught in the present
I am holding it
In my hands
It is very heavy
Very heavy
Please
Help me
To get through

These times in my life
When the earth seems to crumble
Rumble like an earthquake
Spewing disaster
Ground all around
Quaking
Shaking
I reel, I feel unsteady
Drunk with doom, deep in gloom
Distraught
Caught in the web of despair
I must not yield
There is a field
Ahead
Where the ground is still firm
The grass still green
It can be seen
Off in the distance
I must move toward it

Don't be angry at the world. I am, you know.
Angry at the world
I often think of all the tragedies
Here. There.
Everywhere
Tragedies
And I feel ashamed
Can't be angry at the world
   Poor dear world
   Spinning
   Spinning
   Turbulently spinning
   Chaotic
   Befuddled
   Confused
   Groping
Do you know, world
Where you are going?
World
Have you, too, lost your way?

My thoughts are mine alone
Created by my own free will
Pondering. Wondering. Reflecting. Teasing.
Smoldering. Depressing. Rejecting. Pleasing.
Sad. Glad. Tame. Wild.
Thoughts of every kind.
Binding. Winding.
Clasping. Grasping.
From the depths. To the heights.
Thoughts are priceless treasures.
Measures cannot contain thoughts. Thoughts transcend.
Rich. I am so rich. I'm thinking
That I'm rich
With tons and tons of thoughts. Mine alone.
Unless I choose to share. My thoughts.
Cannot really lose my thoughts
Or have them taken from me.
Must hold on.
To my thoughts.

Mind, you're too garrulous. You just go on and on.
Stop thinking. Where does it get you? Stop that
thinking. It's not solving anything. Not coming up with
any brilliant ideas. Just getting to be a bit of a nuisance.
I try to rest. You don't let me.
    Learn to rest. It's best. Everybody needs a rest.
Stop that thinking. That incessant thinking. Rest. Be
still.
    Listen.
    Mind, are you listening? Now mind what I am saying.
Listen.
    Learn to listen.

I must not spend too much time alone
I must not spend too much time in tears
I must not sit back and mope
I must not be afraid to socialize
I must not bemoan my fate
I must not be too self-deprecating
I must not neglect my appearance
I must not neglect my house
I must not neglect my children
I must concentrate on my teaching
I must not be unreasonable
I must not be sorry for myself
I must not remain on the receiving end
I must not expect miracles

Sometimes
I'm in a land
Of dreams
It seems
A land of dreams
I dream that things
Will be all right
Oh, not tonight
No, not tonight
But by tomorrow
There'll be less sorrow
Oh, not tonight
No, not tonight
But by tomorrow
There'll be less sorrow
That's how it seems
In my land of dreams

I see your face
Every place
I see your face

Everywhere
Your face is there

I see your face
I see your face
I'll always see
Your face

How do I miss thee?

I miss sharing
   The air I breathe
   The sky I see
   The trees I see
   The flowers
   The earth around me
I miss sharing
With you
I miss your every word
Your touch
So much
So much

LET GO, MY LOVE
LET GO
 DON'T HOLD ME SO
I KNOW
I KNOW
 BUT JUST A LITTLE
 LET ME GO
JUST A LITTLE
LET ME GO

Part V

No One Ever Promised Us Tomorrow

The second summer has begun. Once again I am wondering how to spend the days. My friends say I should travel. But I am only interested in visiting my family. My dear extended family. Always forming a loving net. Wrapping me in it.

How can I get myself to go off somewhere alone? How can I get over my lassitude? My indifference. The feeling of not really wanting to travel any more.

Anyway, there's so much to do right here. Work in the garden. Get those tomatoes growing. Clean closets. Attend to other chores around the house. Still have so many things to go through. So many neglected things.

And there are friends to see.

Play some bridge. Play some tennis. Drive down to the shore.

Should break the summer up, though. Go somewhere. Where? I really don't have the spark to go. No place I really want to travel. No place. Not really. Still don't want to travel. Not really.

Did you ever go to play tennis
And forget your racquet?
Go for a swim
And forget your suit?
Don't be surprised
Don't be surprised
It's easy to do
Might happen to you
Ask me. I know
I've just done so
Ask me. I know
I've just done so

Dearest, I have destroyed our letters. It was
difficult to do, but after all, they were for you,
and me.

Today, in the NEW YORKER, I read that Jefferson
had made a copy of his "Head and Heart" letter to
Maria Cosway. A copy. Of a love letter. Jefferson
had made a copy. The original letter is long since
gone. The copy survives. So all the world can
see. I guess famous people expect the innermost
aspects of their lives to be examined.

I couldn't bear the thought of sharing with
others what was meant for you and me alone.

So, the letters are gone.

Like you.

Gone.

Where is everybody?
There isn't a sound, no one around
No children playing, no voices saying
   This or that
No shout, no one's out
   And it's Saturday
Guess it's too grey
The quiet almost shrieks
To shatter the stillness
Seeks
To make some noise, undo the sober poise
Of unearthly silence
   Too still, too still
   I think that I will
      Play some Bach to shock the quiet
      That's it
      Play some Bach
      Play some Bach
Unlock
The quiet

Job. When I think of Job. And all others like him. I marvel. What acceptance. What resignation. What patience. Such faith.

Faith. Faith....

They say "It is a tree of life to those who hold it fast, and all who cling to it find happiness. Its ways are pleasantness and all its paths are peace."

I know I haven't reached out for that tree of life. Not at this time. Too much rationalization. Too much intellectualization. Too much of "What's the use?" Too little faith.

I would like to reach out. To learn the meaning. Somehow, something holds me back.

Someday, who knows? Perhaps someday.

As for now, could it really be that after all it's up to me? Which will my companions be? Is it really up to me?

DETERMINATION
VACILLATION

COURAGE
FEAR

SERENITY
UNCERTAINTY

Could it be that after all, it's simply up to me? To choose... Really, is it up to me?

There have been so many changes in my life. I've been plagued with constant uncertainty. Tremulousness. Vagueness. Decisions. Indecision. Ordinary things have seemed so weighty.

Some clarity has come back. Slowly. I'm beginning to think more clearly. Not yet in the old way. Don't know if I'll ever again be able to think in the old way. But I *am* beginning to think. Beginning to find it less arduous to make decisions. Beginning to realize I have choices. Beginning to worry far more about others. Far less about myself.

Emerson said, "We live amid surfaces, and the true art of life is to skate well on them."

Must try to skate well. To adjust to different surfaces. Venture further into my new world. Learn to skate well.

Just got a phone call from Baltimore.

"Come for a visit."

I've been thinking. If I'm ever going to get used to the idea of some longer trips away, traveling alone, I ought to begin to do more things by myself. Get more assurance. Stop being so ambivalent.

I'll go for that visit to Baltimore. Then I'm going off to Washington. By myself. If only for a day. After all, Washington was always such a special place for us. There are so many memories.

I remember that very last weekend we had there, together. It was so soon before the end. We had no way of knowing. It was cold. Wintry. Was that an omen? I recall where we went. Where we walked. What we said.

I want to go back. While I can still remember.

Paths we walked together
I must walk again
Alone
Some because I must
Some because I should
Some because . . . . .
Because . . . . . .
Just because

Now, on my way back home, I feel a little tired, yet a little exhilarated. A little encouraged.

It was pleasant to be in Baltimore. I liked walking down to the waterfront. Saw an old ship in the harbor, the *Samuel Chase*. The *Samuel Chase*! Wasn't that the ship that went to North Africa in 1943, with my loved one on it? And there it was. In the harbor. In Baltimore.

I did go to Washington, too. Walked around. Went into some of the buildings. Some were new. With doors wide open. Inviting me in.

I see there are many things I should try. Go many places. I must not be afraid of being by myself. Work more at being my own person. Stand on my own two feet.

Have been thinking. I can manage. I like being able to manage. I love my little car. I love my little house. I like not being poor, and I don't mind not being rich.

How awful it must be to be both widowed and poor. I am really grateful for what I have. It's enough. More than enough. If I must be a widow. Enough.

If there are meant to be years ahead for me, what will they be like? What will I be like? In the years ahead. Can I really get hold again? Start anew? No way of being sure. I wonder, does everyone feel this way? Just a little insecure? Because there's no way of really being sure.

Must keep on trying to take hold. No slipping back too much. Must fight to keep those spirits up. Take hold.

Went to the Berkshires
Glad that I went
Glad to be back
With my old friends
And now some new
Good to have these new friends, too
Today I was asked to play
Some bridge
With my new friends
Can see the trends
Friends old and new
Old friends and new
Bridge
Build a bridge
That's what I must do

Is this what it's all about?
Is this what it's all about?
You are born
Live in a children's world
Grow up
Marry
Live in a lover's world
Have children
Watch them grow
Lose your Life's mate
Find a new world
A woman's world
Is this what it's all about?
A woman's world?

Women
Women
Women
I am one of you
One of many
One of you
We are living longer
Growing stronger
Determined
Determined
To have strength
Strength
Must have strength
We are women

Today
After all my little chores were done
I sat outside
Out in the sun
The leaves were dancing on the trees
There was such a gentle, gentle breeze
Birds sang a song
Flowers swayed
I prayed
I prayed
Today
Out in the sun
When all my little chores were done
Help me to find
Peace of mind
Help me to find
Peace of mind

Isn't it a lovely day
What a lovely, lovely day
But I must clean the house today
There's lint on the chairs
There's dirt on the stairs
House looks bad
Kind of sad
Must clean the house today
Oh, what's that tone
Must be the phone
Hello, hello, I say
What's on your mind
Today
Of course, of course I'll go with you
Really had nothing at all to do
No need to clean the house
Today
Not on this lovely day
Not on this lovely, lovely day

The yellow primrose in the garden is so bright. So cheerful. The peonies are beyond beauty. Exquisitely perfect. From over the fence, rambling red roses are creeping. The tiger lilies are breathtaking. Yellow thistle. Purple foxglove. Extraordinary. The trees seem greener this year. More beautiful. Wonder why? Everything seems so much more alive. Could I be feeling more alive?

There's a robin. I like robins.

Robin Redbreast, I like the way you hop.

I'm glad you came into my garden.

I like the little park nearby. I like to walk in the
pleasant little park nearby, that little park that lured
us when we were deciding which house we should buy.
Tiny children and bigger ones play for hours in that
park, as our boys used to do. Now the swings and horses
are much more fun, much more imaginative, and there
are those super spin-arounds and climbing
challenges, if one just dares. I would like to dare, but
they'd laugh, the little children would laugh. Well, it's fun
watching, anyway, even if I don't play. It's fun
watching.

I walk down by the pond, to see the ducks. They
are lazily sunning. Some duck in for a swim, gliding
easily over the water, so sure of themselves. Some are
impatient to be fed. They make you laugh a little, those
ducks.

I like the little park nearby.

Visits to museums and weekends away are more frequent. Can think of going to the ballet, alone. Might even try dinner out, alone. Must be making some headway. Fewer cobwebs taking over. My memory is less spotty. Find myself grateful for what is good. Fretting less over the bad. Am beginning to count like a miser, storing up a bountiful hoard for some rainy day. A hoard of good things. For some rainy day.

So the summer is passing.

Feel myself stirring. Entering a new phase of my life. What can I do to make the most of it? If I can, I want to be more than just another widow. I don't want to be just another statistic.

Want to tread new paths. I'm not at all sure if I can. But I'm going to try. To find the way. If I can. Try.

Went sailing today
For the first time
Without you
For the first time
Since we learned
To sail together

How did it feel?
Not quite real
Yet all the day
We sailed
I knew
That
You
Would want me to

In Confucian China long ago
It was considered quite an honor
To be told
How well you look, how old
But here, oh dear
Those wrinkles that I see
Creeping up on me
That show my age
I don't know why, but can't deny
I don't want to be told
My, you're looking old today!
I see myself
Looking in the mirror
Looking at my hair
Looking in the mirror
Pretending I don't care
Do I care?
Do I care?
Do I really care?
I wonder
Do I dare
Change my look
Change my style
Be less grim
Wear a smile

Can it be
A little change in me?
I'm more interested
In what is going on
There seems to be
A little change in me
Can it be
There's a change in me?

Must try to get some project going. Don't mean needlework. Or embroidery. It should be something I haven't tried before. Must develop some new momentum. Find a new challenge. Change of pace.

Must find a project. Don't quite know what. Maybe it will come to me. Some project. Something new. Something to do. A project.

I wonder, could it be? These words I've been writing. These thoughts I've been thinking. What if I tried to put them into a book? Might help me, might help others. Why not try? Write a book.

Could this be the project I've been seeking?

Write a book.

Why not. Don't be afraid.

Why not write a book?

I will not buy the *New York Times*.
Not today
Can't read it through
I've work to do
Must write
Just know
That I
Must write
Can't stop to talk
Can't take a walk
Must write
Just know
That I
Must write
Can't take a call
All
I can do
Is write
Just write
Just write

Lines keep coming back to me
Of words and poems
I used to know
Long ago
   In high school
   And in college, too
   Readings that I had to do
   Essays, stories, poems and plays
Knew so many
Line for line
But I forgot
Now I see
Some keep coming back to me
   More real, I feel
   So much more real
   Than when
   I used to know them
   Long ago

I have this need to dream
Not just in my sleep
But during the day
To get away
To fantasize
To reach for things
Beyond my grasp
And try to make them real

How good that this is so
For well I know
Reality
And all that it implies
So I must dream
And dream
And dream
Or the spirit within me
Dies

"Dot-Dot"
That's what
Stacey calls me
I miss her
Want to see her walk
Want to hear her talk
Hear her say
"Dot-Dot, play"
I bought a little wicker chair
For Stacey
Wonder
Should I bring it there?
See her walk
Hear her talk
Thought that I was home to stay
But Illinois, I'm on my way
Fields of soy beans, corn and hay
Something's pulling me to go
Off to play
With Stacey Jo

I've decided. After Illinois, I'm going to California. Visit my family in Berkeley once again.

Then I'm going to try some new places. Heard that La Jolla is very beautiful, with its twisting juniper trees and massive craggy rocks lording it over the Pacific.

And San Diego. What about that famous zoo? Going there would be a good thing to do. I'll talk to the monkeys. They'll gibber back at me. We'll amuse each other with funny faces.

I think that it is time to go new places.

I think I'd really like to go.

Time. To go.

I'm going to go.

It will be another step. Forward.

Sometimes in the sky
The clouds assume such shapes
One gapes
I saw a school of whales
It made me laugh
What a gaffe
Whales up in the sky
As though
They'd lost their way
That day
And I have seen
Giants, too
Olympian gods
In a realm of blue
Smiling, waving
Passing by
On high
There are all sorts
Of things to see
Clouds send messages to me

149.

Did you ever see fog lifting
Over the San Francisco Bay
It slowly lifts its veil
Giving a glimpse, each time more of a glimpse
As to what really is beneath
New buildings and old
Merged together
In forced friendship
Sun coming through the haze
Showing a blaze
Of color
Buildings, water, sky
Mountains in the distance
In dark relief
The fog in parts, still there
But I think the air
Is slowly clearing
As it is for me

Zoos are fantastic places
So many different kinds
Of faces
People milling all around
Trying to look, to see
Where each of us might be
If our specie were not man
Those bears and chimps, adorable imps
Giraffes, lions, deer
Flamingos
Birds of every kind
I felt such kinship with the animals
Wished that they could speak
Wanted so to seek
That common bond from which we came
Wanted to call out to each by name
"Tell me. Tell me. Are we the same?"

The second summer is ending
I'll soon be wending
My way back to school
Will this be my last year of teaching?
Should I start reaching
For some new career?
Is it too late?
To start a new career?
Is it too late?

I wonder
How can I tell my students
Without sounding as ancient
As Methuselah
That there's more to Life
Than hopping from bed to bed
I shiver just a little
For women and mankind
If they stay blind
To Love
There is a deeper sense
Than just the senses
There's more to Life
Than hopping
From bed to bed
When all is said
There's so much more
To Life
There's so much more
To Love

153.

It is now the in-between season
When summer can't make up its mind
Whether to go away quietly
Without fanfare
Or to angrily stage some wild impetuous tantrum
To remind us it's not all that easy
To bow out gracefully

It has become intensely hot
Unseasonably so
With summer staging
Quite a show
Acting like an abandoned bride
Rudely being tossed aside

It makes me feel a little sorry
For summer
I, too, know
What it is like
To feel abandoned

That sky, that sky after the storm
Clouds. Fascinating clouds.
Each one putting on its most glamorous array
The sun, not to be outdone
Somewhat humiliated at its banishment
Comes forth brazenly, trying once again
To assert its majesty
But the clouds are engaged in a color war
They are enraged, and will not be put aside
So easily
On one side, blues, silvers
On the other, greys, purples
Negotiators in white dart back and forth
Trying to arrive at a compromise
   Unbelievably beautiful
   Frightening
I realize
The storm is not yet over

On the holidays
There are no ways
To brush aside
Memories
That won't subside
Insistent
Pervasive
Inundating

Our anniversary
With you gone
And I
Living on
With memories
The day is cold
Bold and clear
A lone bird
Calls out plaintively
As I call out
To you

The play acting still goes on. The cover-up smile is still there. The inner pain and muffled weeping have still not gone away. Will they ever? Can there be happiness again?

Happiness
Will you ever come back to me?
Will I recognize you?
Will you have changed?
I've changed, too
I wonder
Will I dare
Walk right up to you
Would you recognize me?
Could we forget our old score
Try to be friends
Once more?
Not as before
I know not as before
But could we try, you and I?
Could we try?

Went through some old greeting cards today. Came across one written November 25, 1969. Our anniversary. I had written a poem.

"It is enough for me by day
To walk the same bright earth with him
Enough that over us at night
The same great roof of stars is dim
I do not hope to bind the wind
Or set a fetter on the sea
It is enough to feel his love
Blow like music over me."

So.

Tears.

Tears again.

More tears.

Yet the words were haunting. In the midst of my tears I couldn't help but think of them. How well they were written. Too well. It dawned on me. Looking at the card again, I noticed quotes. The poem was in quotes! No source given.

I started to laugh. Tears streaming down my cheeks. That poem. Must have been Teasdale's. Or Millay's. Wasn't sure. Still not sure. But it wasn't my poem. Not mine.

Laughter. Amidst the tears. That's the way it will be. I guess. Tears. But laughter. Coming through. Laughter.

159.

Wherever I have gone, people have been friendly. They seem to want to talk. Reach out. I think there is a need. Today's speed is just too much. People need some quiet touch. Some sense of sharing. Caring.

I found, too, that others besides myself, had experienced great sadness. Oh, I always knew this to be true, of course, but it had never really penetrated fully, been as significant as it now is to me. Others, too, go through so much.

I am also aware, so much more aware, that sooner or later, people must learn to live alone.

And I realize more deeply that beautiful things in our life can hurt That we pay a price for beauty.

I am beginning to have just a little greater understanding of what life is all about.

Life is living
Life is loving
Life is receiving
Life is leaving
Life is joy
Life is sorrow
AND NO ONE EVER
PROMISED US TOMORROW

Time
Has helped
As everyone said
No denying
There's still some crying
And that pain
Still won't go away
But I can face each day
Sometimes with a smile
And while
It isn't always real
I feel
That Time has helped
Time
Has helped

My love
I have not forgotten
Not for a moment
Not for a day
But in a different way
You stay
With me
You see
I am somewhat different now
I had to learn
To free myself a little
To gain some strength at length
To walk by myself
In the living world
But in the secret lair
Within my soul
You know how much I care
My love
You know
How much I care

It took
So much
To write this book
To show my fears
Reveal my tears
To bare my sorrow
And yet I know
It has helped me grow
Each line I wrote, each page
Has pushed me through
Another stage
Made me feel
That I could deal
With what's ahead
Made me feel
That I *must* deal
With what's ahead
Made me feel
That I *can* deal
With what's ahead

Zig Zag
It's been a zig zag
Back and forth
This way, and that
Ahead. Fall back
Zig zag.

Be brave
Be scared
This book I've dared
Feel sad
Feel glad
Zig zag
Back and forth
Zig zag
That's how it's been
Zig zag

Let's laugh awhile
Let's play awhile
And put away
Our fears

There's time to laugh
There's time to cry
There's a time to live
And a time to die

Would you be proud
My love
I'm trying
Really trying
To do
What you
Would want me to
I'm trying
Really trying
Would you be proud
My love?

Index of First Lines

Part I
DEATH IN WINTER

	Page
There's nothing to be said . . .	3
I'd have followed you . . .	4
Dreary . . .	5
A plaintive call . . .	6
We are mortal . . .	7
Who am I? . . .	8
Sometimes I wish . . .	9
That old, old clock . . .	10
Turned in the M.D. plates . . .	11
I must get back to school . . .	12
There are records to keep . . .	13
Weird feeling . . .	14
Should I move . . .	15
If only there were someone . . .	16
Hard to fall asleep . . .	17
Have to go through so many things . . .	18
Am tired . . .	19
Hear the wind . . .	20
I must learn to build a little wall . . .	21
No matter how hard I try . . .	22
I see, and don't see . . .	23
Seems I can't help brooding . . .	24
Despair . . .	25
Drowning . . .	26
Death . . .	27
Oh, my love . . .	28
I promise . . .	29

Part II
THE FIRST SPRING AND SUMMER

Strange . . .   33
How much I wish . . .   34
Your son, Mom . . .   35
Absent-minded . . .   36
Sometimes I feel . . .   37
Not well . . .   38
Just knowing there won't be . . .   39
When you were little ones . . .   40
His presence is everywhere . . .   41
Spring . . .   42
Wool gathering . . .   43
He had that zest for life . . .   44
Think I'll take up bridge again . . .   45
Haven't played tennis in years . . .   46
First time in New York . . .   47
The weekends . . .   48
Drifting . . .   49
Be still, my soul . . .   50
I'm home . . .   51
Weeds . . .   52
Oh well, laugh . . .   53
Everyone has been so kind . . .   54
At times this past winter . . .   55
Each night . . .   56
If I could just phone you . . .   57

Part III
THE LEAVES ARE FALLING

Leaves . . .   61
Widow . . .   62
My heart . . .   63
It's almost dinner time . . .   64

I am afraid . . .   65
Those neighbors in the stucco house . . .   66
I'm going off to the library . . .   67
Thanksgiving . . .   68
Unexpectedly, just like that . . .   69
I'm such a dodo bird . . .   70
There's still a long way to go . . .   71
Take a walk . . .   72
Pleasant . . .   73
Always a circle . . .   74
Afraid people will criticize me . . .   75
Cover that layer of sadness . . .   76
Off, take off my mask . . .   77
Looks as though . . .   78
Pain so deep . . .   79
Complaining? . . .   80
What did I do today? . . .   81
There's something I must tell you . . .   82
So many times each day . . .   83
Outside the gate . . .   84
I dare you . . .   85
Staring out at the Pacific . . .   86
The ocean . . .   87
Ebb and flow . . .   88
What choices do I have? . . .   89
Keep those spirits up . . .   90

Part IV
THIS YEAR HAS PASSED AT LAST

This year has passed . . .   93
Look, it's sleeting . . .   94
Sometimes I do some cross-stitching . . .   95
Those old brass train lamps . . .   96
Thinking back about my education . . .   97
I learned to cook for you . . .   98

169.

At times . . .   99
There were moments of anger . . .   100
You looked into my eyes . . .   101
Part of what I am . . .   102
Close, so close . . .   103
How long the evenings are . . .   104
I'm still in love . . .   105
Remarry . . .   106
I go through the motions . . .   107
I am lonely . . .   108
It is creeping up again . . .   109
The sky is very blue today . . .   110
Let me through . . .   111
These times in my life . . .   112
Don't be angry at the world . . .   113
My thoughts are mine alone . . .   114
Mind, you're too garrulous . . .   115
I must not spend too much time alone . . .   116
Sometimes I'm in a land of dreams . . .   117
I see your face . . .   118
How do I miss thee? . . .   119
Let go, my love . . .   120

Part V
NO ONE EVER PROMISED US TOMORROW

The second summer has begun . . .   123
Did you ever go to play tennis? . . .   124
Dearest, I have destroyed our letters . . .   125
Where is everybody? . . .   126
Job . . .   127
There have been so many changes . . .   128
Just got a phone call from Baltimore . . .   129
Now, on my way back home . . .   130
Have been thinking . . .   131
Went to the Berkshires . . .   132

170.

Is this what it's all about?...   133
Women...   134
Today ..   135
Isn't it a lovely day...   136
The yellow primrose in the garden...   137
I like the little park nearby...   138
Visits to museums and weekends away...   139
Went sailing today...   140
In Confucian China long ago...   141
Can it be?...   142
Must try to get some project going...   143
I will not buy *The New York Times*...   144
Lines keep coming back to me...   145
I have this need to dream...   146
"Dot-dot"...   147
I've decided...   148
Sometimes in the sky...   149
Did you ever see fog lifting?...   150
Zoos are fantastic places...   151
The second summer is ending...   152
I wonder...   153
It is now the in-between-season...   154
That sky, that sky after the storm...   155
On the holidays...   156
Our anniversary...   157
The play acting still goes on...   158
Went through some old greeting cards...   159
Wherever I have gone...   160
Time...   161
My love...   162
It took so much...   163
Zig zag...   164
Let's laugh awhile...   165
Would you be proud?...   166